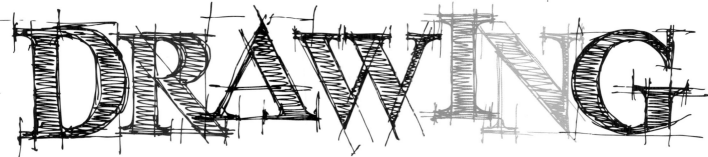

# DRAWING
# SKILLS LAB

**SANDEE EWASIUK**

**CRABTREE**
PUBLISHING COMPANY
WWW.CRABTREEBOOKS.COM

# ART SKILLS LAB

**Author**
Sandee Ewasiuk

**Editors**
Marcia Abramson, Reagan Miller

**Photo research**
Melissa McClellan

**Cover/Interior Design**
T.J. Choleva

**Project Designer**
Sandee Ewasiuk

**Proofreader**
Crystal Sikkens

**Production coordinator
and Prepress technician**
Tammy McGarr

**Print coordinator**
Katherine Berti

Developed and produced for
Crabtree Publishing by
BlueApple*Works* Inc.

**Consultant**
Trevor Hodgson
Fine artist and former director of The Dundas Valley School of Art

**Art & Photographs**
Shutterstock.com: © Excellent backgrounds (background); © Lyudmila Suvorova
(title page background, p. 6 top middle); Iurii Kachkovskyi (p. 4 top right);
© Magnia (p. 5 top right); © basel101658 (p. 5 middle right); © V J Matthew
(p. 6 top left); © James John Harris (p. 6 top right); © Room's Studio (p. 6 middle
right); © Burhan Bunardi (p. 6 bottom left); © Mega Pixel (p. 6 middle bottom);
© MeteeChaicharoen (p. 6 bottom right); © DenisNata (p. 14 top left); © Xarlyxa
(p. 15 bottom right); © Valua Vitaly (p. 16 top); © Makc (p. 25 bottom right);
© Jenelle Jacks (p. 27 top right); © Evgeny Glazunov (p. 28 top)
p. 4 left © Sam Taylor

Instructive paintings © Sandee Ewasiuk cover, p. 5 bottom;
p. 7– 29 excluding bios
p. 13 © Henry Moore reproduced by permission of The Henry Moore Foundation
p. 17 Leonardo Da Vinci/courtesy of www.leonardoda-vinci.org/Public Domain
p. 19 Edgar Degas/Public Domain/Digital image courtesy of the Getty's Open
Content Program
p. 21 Vincent van Gogh/Public Domain/Van Gogh Museum, Amsterdam (Vincent
van Gogh Foundation)
p. 23 Emily Carr/National Gallery of Canada/Purchased 1946
p. 27 John French Sloan/Public Domain/Collection Walker Art Center; Gift of the
T.B. Walker Foundation, Gilbert M. Walker Fund, 1948

**Library and Archives Canada Cataloguing in Publication**

Ewasiuk, Sandee, author
    Drawing skills lab / Sandee Ewasiuk.

(Art skills lab)
Includes index.
Issued in print and electronic formats.
ISBN 978-0-7787-5221-9 (hardcover).--
ISBN 978-0-7787-5234-9 (softcover).--
ISBN 978-1-4271-2178-3 (HTML)

    1. Drawing--Technique--Juvenile literature.
2. Drawing--Juvenile literature. I. Title.

NC655.E93 2018      j741.2      C2018-905548-0
                               C2018-905549-9

**Library of Congress Cataloging-in-Publication Data**

Names: Ewasiuk, Sandee, author.
Title: Drawing skills lab / Sandee Ewasiuk.
Description: New York, New York : Crabtree Publishing, [2019] |
   Series: Art skills lab | Includes index.
Identifiers: LCCN 2018050538 (print) | LCCN 2018056560 (ebook) |
   ISBN 9781427121783 (Electronic) |
   ISBN 9780778752219 (hardcover : alk. paper) |
   ISBN 9780778752349 (pbk. : alk. paper)
Subjects: LCSH: Drawing--Technique--Juvenile literature. |
   Design--Technique--Juvenile literature. | Artists--Biography--
   Juvenile literature.
Classification: LCC NC655 (ebook) | LCC NC655 .E93 2019 (print) |
   DDC 741.2--dc23
LC record available at https://lccn.loc.gov/2018050538

## Crabtree Publishing Company

www.crabtreebooks.com      1-800-387-7650

Printed in the U.S.A./012019/CG20181123

**Published in Canada
Crabtree Publishing**
616 Welland Ave.
St. Catharines, Ontario
L2M 5V6

**Published in the United States
Crabtree Publishing**
PMB 59051
350 Fifth Avenue, 59th Floor
New York, New York 10118

**Published in the United Kingdom
Crabtree Publishing**
Maritime House
Basin Road North, Hove
BN41 1WR

**Published in Australia
Crabtree Publishing**
Unit 3 – 5 Currumbin Court
Capalaba
QLD 4157

# CONTENTS

# GET INTO DRAWING

Approach this book with a sense of adventure! It is designed to unleash the creativity that exists within you! The projects in this book will help you express your feelings, your thoughts, and your ideas through your art. Create images of things you want to say and messages you want to share. Find your own individual style and run with it!

DRAWING AND SEEING

To be able to draw well you must be able to observe things well. Drawing helps you learn how to look at the world around you. You can look at an apple and see a fruit, but when drawing you will see a round form with light and shadows, a sharp edge, and color.

### MINI-BIOGRAPHIES

Throughout the book you will find mini-biographies highlighting the work of well-known artists. You can learn a lot about drawing **techniques** by looking at great works of art. Experiment with the techniques the artists used. Examine each artwork to see how its parts were put together, and how **symmetry**, types of lines, and color were used.

# DESIGN ELEMENTS WHEN DRAWING

The elements of design include line, shape, texture, pattern, and composition. Artists use these elements in different ways to achieve the result they want.

Line is the edge between two colors or shapes. It does not have to be straight! Lines can go in any direction and come in any shape, length, or thickness. Artists use lines to draw the viewer's eye in the direction they want it to go.

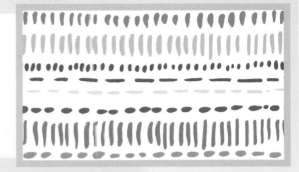

Shape is any enclosed space in a painting. A shape's edges may be created by lines, textures, or colors.

Physical texture describes the surface of the artwork, such as smooth or rough.

Pattern is the way colors or shapes are combined and repeated to create a special effect, such as contrast or movement.

Composition is the arrangement of all the shapes, lines, colors, spaces, and textures in a drawing. Artists carefully use these elements so viewers' eyes will follow a path leading to the key, or most important, element or message of the work.

# MATERIALS AND COLORS

All the projects in this book can be done with pens, pencils, charcoal, pastels, and markers. A large pad of drawing paper will be needed as well. Different drawing materials create different effects. Read below to learn more about drawing materials you will use in this book.

Dry Pastels

Oil Pastels

### Graphite pencils
**Varieties/Types:**
*Choose very soft graphites to create dark shades. Use hard graphites to create lighter shades.*

### Colored pencils
*Colored pencils can be blended and layered together to create different shades and colors.*

### Pastels
**Varieties/Types:**
*Dry pastels create a chalk-like effect. Oil pastels have rich color and do not dry.*

### Charcoal
*Charcoal is used in art for drawing and making rough sketches.*

### Eraser
*A kneaded eraser removes marks gently from paper without a lot of rubbing.*

### Tip
Charcoal and pastels can be messy so set up a workstation with newspapers to protect the table. You might want to wear an art smock and have a wet cloth to clean your hands.

### What Surface To Draw On?
You can use a variety of different paper for drawing on. Drawing paper comes in different textures and different weights. Below is a chart showing which drawing materials are best suited for certain papers.

| Drawing Materials | Drawing Paper |
| --- | --- |
| Colored and graphite pencils | semi-smooth paper |
| Markers and pens | smooth paper |
| Pastels and charcoal | heavyweight, rough paper |

### Pencil sharpener
*Both colored and graphite pencils work best when sharp, so it is a good idea to always have a good pencil sharpener with you when sketching.*

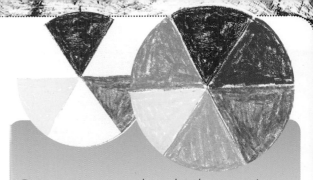

## Using Color When Drawing

Artists use the color wheel as a tool to help them mix colors. A color wheel is a diagram that shows how colors are related. A simple color wheel is divided into two types of colors: **primary** and **secondary**. The **primary colors** are red, blue, and yellow. They are called primary because they are the only three colors that can't be made from others. **Secondary colors** are made by mixing two primary colors together.

## Complementary Colors

When choosing colors for a drawing, remember that colors from opposite sides of the wheel **complement**, or balance, each other. For example, red and green, yellow and violet, and blue and orange are complementary colors.

## Value in Drawings

In art, value refers to the lightness or darkness of colors. Values are used to create highlights and shadows in a drawing because the role of value is to create the illusion of light. In black and white drawings the values are applied by using **hatching** or tonal drawing as explained on pages 20–21 and 22–23.

*Highlights and shadows created by the hatching technique*

*The value scale is a system of organizing values. It has values of white and black at each end, and shades of gray in between. Together, the shades of gray help create the illusion of depth. Make a value scale using a selection of drawing pencils and drawing paper. Draw a rectangle and divide it into nine equally sized boxes. Start with black at one end and white at the other. Draw a **mid-tone** in the middle and work your way to both ends.*

White ← → Black

*Draw your own color wheel to practice mixing colors. Draw a circle and divide it into 6 equal pie shapes. Use oil pastels to color the primary colors first. Mix red and yellow to create orange. Mix red and blue to create violet. Mix yellow and blue to create green.*

## Warm and Cool Colors

The color wheel also can be divided into warm and cool colors. Artists use cool and warm colors to express emotions in their art. Warm colors such as red, yellow, and orange are bright and come forward to meet our eye. If you want something to stand out use warm colors. Cool colors such as blue, violet, and green are more calming. Using both creates **depth** in a drawing.

### Try This!

To create different values in colored drawings you can mix colors to make colors lighter or darker. This creates different shades and tints. Adding black to any color creates a **shade**. For example, adding black to red makes maroon. Adding white to any color creates a **tint**. Adding white to red creates pink. Adding gray to a color creates a **tone**.

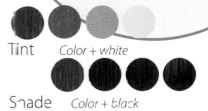

Tint    *Color + white*

Shade    *Color + black*

# DOODLE AWAY!

**Doodling** can be a great warm-up exercise before you start drawing your art. It is a great way to practice making lines, thin marks, flowing lines, and thick lines. When you doodle you can relax and be creative at the same time. Doodle away and get comfortable with making scribbles, hatching, and different types of lines and tones.

## You Will Need:
- Smooth paper
- Markers

## PROJECT GUIDES

1. Doodle some hearts using one color.

2. Doodle some spirals, circles, and curvy lines using two complementary colors.

3. Doodle a city scene in one color. Your scene might include buildings, streets, and cars.

4. Doodle some flowers using three colors.

5. Doodle some faces in a variety of colors.

6. Fill an entire page with doodles in many colors. Fill the page until there is very little white space left. Color the doodles.

### Try This!
Use the doodling exercise to get familiar with the color concepts explained on page 7. Doodle in one of the primary colors of your choice to create **monochromatic** art. Try to create green by using a yellow marker to draw over an area colored in blue. Then test the complementary colors. When used together, they will seem to bounce off of one another. Do one doodle in red and green, one using yellow and violet colors, and another one using blue and orange markers. Do they look brighter to you when used next to each other?

**4**

**5**

**6**

## Helpful Tips

*When you doodle, you're doing more than making art. Scientists have found that doodling improves concentration and lowers stress! Here are some tips for great doodling:*

- *Instead of writing down a list, doodle it! You could doodle the art supplies you need, for example.*

- *Make a doodle using just words for a whole different look.*

- *Experiment with your pencil. Use the tip and the sides. Try it both dull and sharp.*

- *Use all kinds of lines, curves, and shapes.*

- *Doodle in black and white and in color. How does each one make you feel?*

# IT'S ALL ABOUT THE CONTOURS

Contour is a French word meaning an "outline." It is a drawing technique to capture the most basic form of a **subject**. This is one of the first ways that we learn how to draw. There are several different types of contour line drawings. Get familiar with the different types of line drawings and then try drawing on your own. Each drawing method encourages your eyes, hand, and brain to work together.

**You Will Need:**
- Sketch pad or drawing paper
- Pencil

## BLIND CONTOUR DRAWING

*Sometimes artists will make a drawing without ever looking at their paper. They keep their eyes closely focused on the details of their subject while they draw. This is called blind contour drawing. It helps artists focus on both basic shapes and fine details while improving their hand-eye coordination.*

1  Look outside at some birds. Draw a contour drawing of a bird.

2  Try drawing a bird again, but this time don't look down at your drawing.

1

2
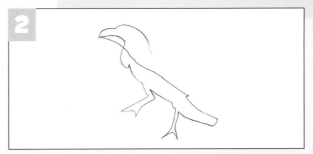

## CONTINUOUS LINE DRAWING

*Continuous line drawing means that the pencil never leaves the paper. The drawing is one unbroken line. Blind contour and continuous line drawing are often done together. It's not easy, but it's a great way to boost your coordination and observation skills.*

3  Start by drawing your hand as it lies flat on a table. Don't lift your pencil while drawing the line.

4  Look at your hands and draw their shape in one continuous line. Do not lift the pencil off the paper unless you go off the edge of the paper.

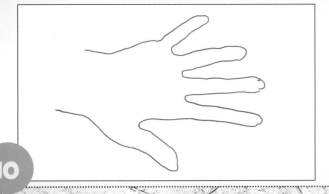

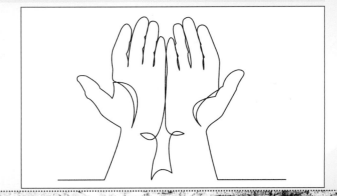

## CROSS CONTOUR DRAWING

*Cross contours are drawn lines that wrap around an object. They may be vertical, horizontal, curved, or angled. Cross contours look like the contour lines on a map, and they work the same way. They create a 3-D effect and add energy and movement to a drawing.*

## Try This!

Try doing a contour drawing of the same subject in several ways. Draw one from memory. Draw another one while looking at the subject. Try doing a contour drawing with your **non-dominant hand**. How do all these drawings compare? Some of these drawings might not look like the subject but might still be very interesting. All of these exercises are great for improving your drawing skills.

**5** Find an object around the house and draw an outline shape of that object.

**6** Take your object drawing and start drawing curved **parallel** lines across the object. These cross contour lines will give the object a form and make it seem more dimensional.

**7** Draw cross contour lines on your hand drawing. To show the raised surface of the hand on the table, draw the line from one edge of the paper to the other. When drawing across the hand make the line curve.

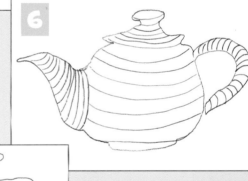

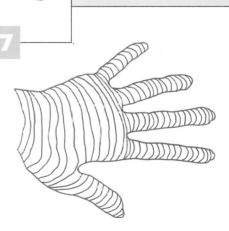

## Helpful Tips

● *Take all the time you need. Observe carefully. You may want to close one eye to do this!*

● *Choose a subject that you can draw life-size or close to it.*

● *Tape your paper to your drawing surface so it stays in place.*

# SCRIBBLE ART

Take your continuous line drawing skills further. In this exercise, you will draw with a pen or marker to release your creativity. No judging or erasing allowed. The drawing will be fluid and continuous. The idea is to draw an **outline** and shade in parts of the outline without lifting your pen. Experiment with different ways of making continuous lines.

## You Will Need:

- Smooth paper
- Pencil or pens
- Colored pencils

## PROJECT GUIDES

1. Do a scribble warm-up exercise. Scribble until your scribbles are very loose. There should be no tension left, just easy scribbles. This will release your creativity.

2. Practice making more controlled scribbles, such as zigzag lines, curvy lines, tight circles, and loose circles. Try it with colored pencils, pens, and markers.

3. Use a photo or real-life subject for reference. Don't lift your pen until you are finished. See how much of the object you can draw before you lift your pen.

4. For a more controlled scribbling piece, start by scribbling an outline.

5. Continue scribbling and fill in some of the details.

6. You can switch colors and continue drawing as needed.

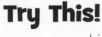

## Try This!

Observe your subject closely as you draw, and check your paper only when you start a new line. Switch hands to see how that feels. Don't think about how it looks. These exercises will improve your **hand-eye-mind coordination**.

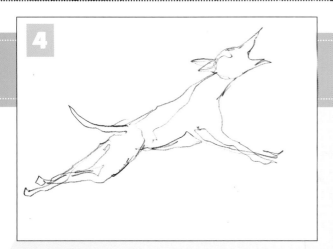

**4**

**5**

**6**

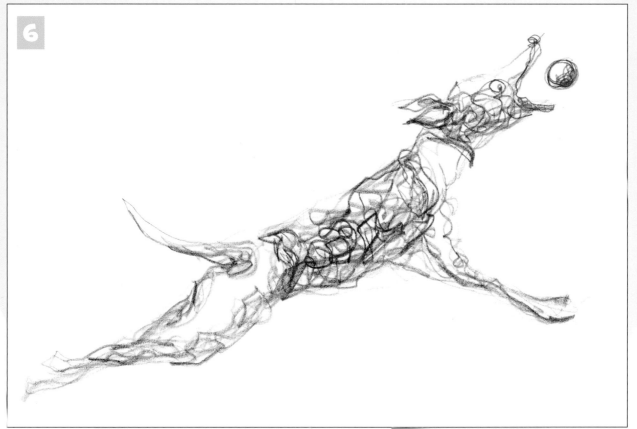

## HENRY MOORE

(1898–1986) England

Henry Moore became famous for abstract sculptures, but he never stopped making realistic drawings of the natural world. He could see flocks of sheep from his studio window and often sketched them. "I began to realize that underneath all that wool was a body, which moved in its own way," he wrote. He drew with a ballpoint pen. Rather than working from an outline, he used swirls and zigzags to capture the energy and personality of a living animal.

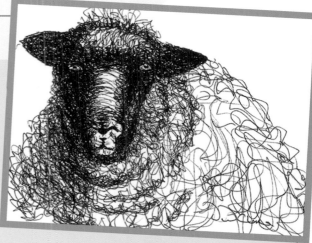

Moore drew *Head* in 1974.

# DRAWING WITH SHAPES

You can draw a cat by sketching an outline, but another way to approach drawing is to draw the shapes that together form the subject of your drawing. Look closely at any subject and you will see some basic shapes that join together within it. Breaking the subject into shapes can be a helpful way to start a drawing.

## You Will Need:

- Photo of cat
- Paper
- Pencil
- Colored pencils
- Eraser

## PROJECT GUIDES

**1** Find a photo of a cat and print a copy of it. Use a pencil to draw the shapes that make up the cat's body.

**2** Use a pencil to draw these shapes on a separate piece of paper.

**3** On a new piece of paper, begin drawing the cat's body using the shapes from your second paper as a guide.

**4** Draw an outline around the shapes and erase some of the lines that overlapped. Add details such as whiskers, a mouth, and claws. Add shading on the face and body to show the markings on the cat's fur.

**5** Color the drawing with colored pencils. Add texture by using short strokes of pencil.

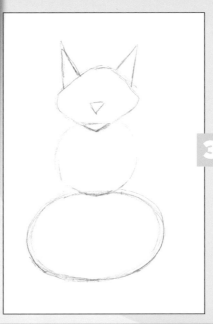

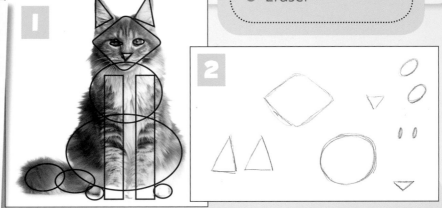

*Good shapes to use when drawing characters are ovals, circles, and rounded rectangles. Try mixing and matching the shapes to best fit your character's outline.*

A long oval shape

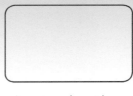

A rectangle with rounded corners

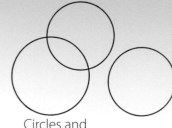

Circles and overlapping circles

**4**

**5**

# Try This!

Basic shapes are the foundation of many drawings. Practice looking for shapes that make up the subjects in other drawings. Even the detailed octopus shown below can be drawn using basic shapes.

**Done**

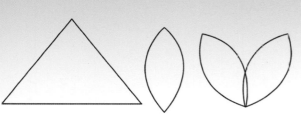

A triangle          Petal shapes          S-shapes

# GRID HEAD

To draw a **realistic portrait**, it is important that a person's features be in **alignment** and **proportion**. Using a grid can be helpful for this type of drawing. With practice, you will be able to **visualize** the grid and not have to draw it.

## PROJECT GUIDES

**1** Find a photo of a person that you can draw on. Choose a photo where the person's head is facing forward and they are looking directly at the camera.

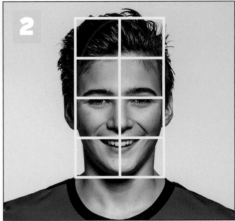

**2** On the photo, sketch an oval shape for the head. Draw a rectangle over the oval. Draw a horizontal line to divide the rectangle in half. You now have two squares. Draw a horizontal line to divide the top square in half. Do the same to divide the bottom square. Notice how all the facial features line up with this grid.

**3** On paper draw an oval again. Lightly draw the same grid on top of it. Draw ears starting at line B. Draw the neck coming from the ears in a curving line.

**4** – Draw the eyes at line B or halfway down the oval.
– Draw eyebrows above the eyes.
– Draw the nose from line B to line C using the center vertical line as a guide.
– Draw the mouth just below line C. The bottom lip is almost always fuller than the top lip.
– Draw hair from the top of the oval to line A.

**5** Finish the portrait by erasing the grid. Add some details and shading.

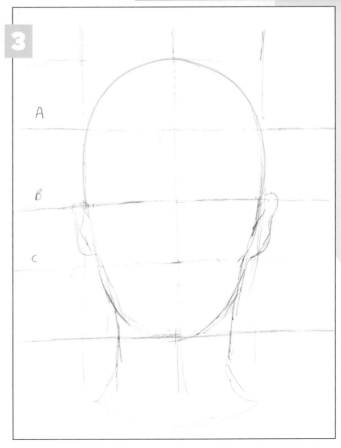

**4**

A

B

C

**5**

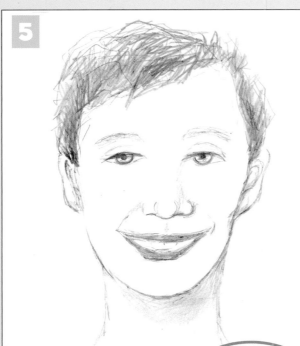

## Try This!
Draw a more lively portrait by ignoring proportion. Make some features too large or small. Try to capture the spirit of the person!

○·· **LEONARDO DA VINCI** ···O

(1452–1519) Republic of Florence (present-day Italy)

Leonardo da Vinci was a master of drawing, painting, and sculpture. He filled many journals with sketches of all the subjects that fascinated him. One of those subjects was **anatomy**. He studied and practiced drawing different parts of the body including faces, hands, muscles, and bones. He used the grid method to help make sure his drawings were in correct proportion. Some of his sketches are so perfect that they are still used in medical schools today!

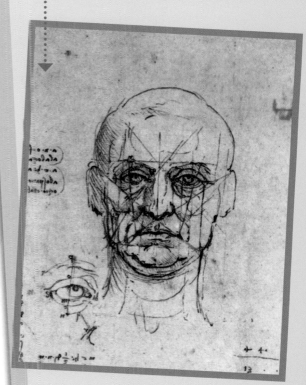

Facial drawing, 1489-1490

# STOP ACTION

Gestural drawing is a technique that attempts to capture motion and energy. It is used to show accurate appearance and details, and also movement. You want to capture the line of action. This is an imaginary line that runs through the spine of a figure. The action line shows movement. When a line curves, it draws the viewer along the action. Some sketches even have more than one line of action if different parts of the subject are moving.

## You Will Need:

- Paper
- Pencil
- Colored pencils
- Eraser

## PROJECT GUIDES

1. Get a friend to pose for you or look at photos online. Sketch a person standing. Sketch only the action lines. Do not worry about details. Sketch a person jumping.

2. Sketch a person running. Capture the motion. Observe where their arms are. Where is the head located? Is it leaning forward?

3. Sketch a person playing soccer. Observe where the joints are. Where do they bend? Transfer what you see to action lines.

4. Sketch a person jumping in the air. Observe the legs and arms. How do they move in relation to the body?

5. Sketch a person dancing. Try to capture the joy of dancing in the action line. Choose your favorite action sketch and turn it into a finished drawing. Start drawing the clothes. Make the feet and hands look more realistic. Erase some of the action lines as you go.

6. Use light colored pencils to fill in the person. Shade with darker colored pencils.

7. Draw a face.

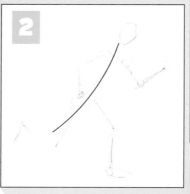

## Helpful Tips

*When you choose to capture motion, sketch repeatedly and on the top of previous images. Work quickly to capture the moment. Great artists such as Edgar Degas could draw a series of poses in a short amount of time, often as little as a few seconds.*

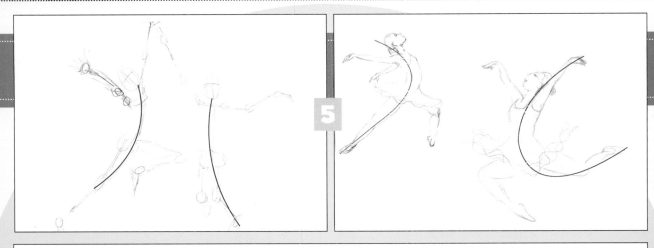

**5**

**6**

## Try This!

Ask a friend or family member to get into a sports pose, such as shooting a basketball. Draw a quick sketch and find the action lines. Try different poses. What do they have in common?

## EDGAR DEGAS

(1834–1917) France

Edgar Degas is known for capturing both the motion and emotion of a moment in his drawings, paintings, and sculptures. He was fascinated by the grace and power of dancers, and he drew them more than a thousand times! His ballerinas are full of action lines and seem ready to dance off the page or canvas. Some are even partly cut off at the edge. He liked to use unusual angles or focus, such as a dancer with her back to the viewer, to create a lifelike feeling. For the same reason, he sometimes drew a dancer scratching her back or ironing a costume.

*Ballet Dancers Rehearsing,* about 1877

# HATCH THAT

Now that you have learned to draw the outline of a subject, the next step is to add shading to give the object depth and to make it appear three-dimensional. It is the difference between a circle and a ball. You can change a circle into a ball by adding shadows and highlights. Shading is created by making marks on the outline. These marks are called hatching and they will bring your drawing to life.

## You Will Need:

- Paper
- Pencil
- Colored pencils
- Pen

## PROJECT GUIDES

**1** Practice parallel hatching which is drawing straight lines parallel and close to each other.

**2** Practice cross hatching which is drawing straight lines parallel and close to each other, and then more straight lines in the opposite direction. This creates a more dense shading.

**3** Practice contour hatching which is just like cross hatching but the lines are curved to match the subject. It can be done as parallel hatching or cross hatching. The key is to follow the **contour** of what you are drawing. This method of hatching can make your drawing look less flat.

**4** Sketch an outline of an animal or stuffed toy in pencil.

**5** Go over the pencil outline with a dark pen. Start shading sections of the outline using parallel hatching and cross hatching. Hatch only one side of the object. Imagine the light coming from the right so that everything on the left is in shade. That is where you will apply the hatching.

**6** Apply more hatching to the shaded areas to bring the sketch to life.

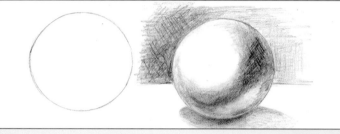

## Try This!

Another form of shading is called **stippling**. Stippling uses tiny dots to create a shadow. Try drawing the same subject, but use stippling rather than hatching to create shaded areas.

## VINCENT VAN GOGH

(1853–1890) Netherlands

Like many great painters, Vincent van Gogh believed that visual art starts with a drawing. He studied form and movement by making more than a thousand drawings in his short life. He often began with a pencil, or a special pen made from a reed, and then applied ink with a brush. He used stippling, cross hatching, and many slashes and **whorls**. His drawings show how he developed the bold strokes that have made his paintings famous.

*Barn Owl Viewed from the Side,* 1877

# TONAL SHADE

Tonal values are the lightness or darkness of an object. They are created by the way light falls. Areas of strong light are called highlights and darker areas are shadows.

Shading is the way an artist uses highlights and shadows. Charcoal is great for experimenting with shading techniques using different ranges of light to dark values. Charcoal drawings can be full of light, shadows, and depth. You can also remove tone with an eraser.

## You Will Need:

- Rough drawing paper
- Charcoal pencil
- Vine or compressed charcoal
- Kneaded eraser

## PROJECT GUIDES

**1** On a small piece of paper, make a tonal scale, from light to dark, using vine or compressed charcoal. Use different pressure to create different tones.

**2** Use a charcoal pencil to lightly draw an outline of an apple. Draw a horizon line as well.

**3** Cover the top part of the paper with a light coating of charcoal.

**4** Start filling in the apple with charcoal. Use your finger to blend the edges of the different tones. Try to have many different tones and different shades. Imagine a light source coming from one direction. It lights the top of the apple but the bottom is in shade.

**5** Make a pattern in the foreground. Drag the eraser through the dark charcoal to create lines.

**6** Use the eraser to create lighter tones by removing some of the charcoal. Smooth out the top background by rubbing a piece of scrunched-up paper towel over it. Draw a shadow under the apple.

**1**

**2**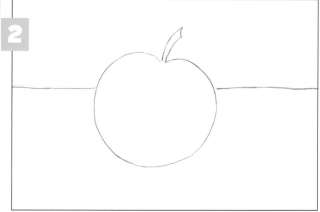

## Helpful Tips

- *Put a piece of paper over the drawing to rest your hand and prevent smudging.*

- *When shading around a shape, leave a little line of light color at the edge. It will help to make the object look dimensional rather than flat.*

**3**

**4**

**5**

**6**

## Try This!

Practice shading by drawing a hollow object like a teacup or coffee mug. The light looks different as it enters the hollow inside. Use highlights and shadows to show the different values. You can even have the cup cast a shadow.

*Wood Interior* c. 1931-1933

### EMILY CARR
(1871–1945) Canada

Emily Carr used tints, shades, and perspective to create her dreamlike landscapes. She loved the Pacific Northwest and wanted Canadian art to have its own style with a strong connection to nature. She used charcoal for sketches to get a feel for her subject. Charcoal allowed her to play with shadows and light. To show the beauty of the forest, she often chose an interesting perspective, such as drawing from the ground looking up.

# THE SPACE BETWEEN

A drawing has two kinds of space: negative and positive. Positive space contains the subject or subjects of the drawing. Negative space is all the rest, whether it is around or between subjects, or between a subject and the edge of the page. Understanding how negative and positive spaces work together will improve your drawings. In this exercise, decide on what appears to be the main area of negative space around the subject. Fill the negative space with colors to create the background image. The subject, or the positive space, will appear as a clear shape in the middle.

## You Will Need:
- Object to draw
- Paper
- Colored pencils

## PROJECT GUIDES

**1** Find an object around the house that has a simple shape, such as this wooden duck.

**2** Draw a contour drawing of the object. Now look at your drawing and identify the negative and positive space.

**3** Now try to fill in the negative space with only one, light color. You have to pay very close attention to the shape of the object.

**4** Continue filling in the negative space until you are left with only the positive space, or the subject of your drawing. It will appear as a clear area showing only the color of the paper you're drawing on.

**5** Use other colors to show water, shadow under the subject, and the background. The exercise can end here or you can go on to step 6.

**6** Color in the positive space adding details to the subject so it is easier to identify.

**1**

**2**

**3**

4

5

6

## Try This!

What do you see when you look at the image on the right? Most people say they see two blue faces in **profile** on an orange background. But other people see an orange goblet on a blue background. The positive and negative spaces have switched!

This famous optical illusion, called Rubin's vase, has fascinated people for more than a century. It also has an important lesson for artists. Positive and negative space are shapes that interact with each other.

Now make your own optical illusion:

- Find a large profile picture of a person in a magazine and cut it out following the profile outline.
- Trace the outline of your magazine cutout on a colored piece of paper. Cut out the profile shape from the colored paper. Do it twice, you will need two profile shapes of the same color for the project.
- Get a sheet of paper for the background. Make sure your background paper is a different color than your profile cutouts.
- Place the profile cutouts on your background sheet. Flip one cutout so that the profile shapes face each other as shown on the picture above.
- Once you have them positioned, glue the cutouts to the background sheet.

Ask your friends and family what they see!

# OVERLAPPING FISH

Create a drawing of a fish aquarium using oil pastels. You can create the illusion of space by overlapping objects. Draw objects in the foreground larger than those in the background to create depth. Oil pastels are great for blending colors together. Use this technique to make the fish look colorful and interesting.

**You Will Need:**
- Pastel paper
- Pencil
- Chalk pastels

## PROJECT GUIDES

**1** Many large aquariums have live webcams online where you can view fish swimming. View one of these live webcams and get a feel for the way the fish move in their environment. Make some sketches of what you remember. Draw fish in the foreground larger than fish in the background. Overlap some of the fish and plants. This will create a sense of depth.

**2** Choose your favorite sketch. Draw the same sketch on the dark pastel paper. Add more details to the sketch.

**3** Choose the colors that you are going to use. Practice drawing on a spare piece of paper to get a feel for the pressure needed to make the colors look bold.

**4** Use the pastels to roughly color in all the outlines.

**5** Make the fish look more realistic by applying different values of colors. Use light-colored pastels and create highlights to give the fish a more three-dimensional look. Blend the pastels together with your finger.

**6** Continue adding more details. Use the edge of the pastel to make lines. Use dark-colored pastels to create shadows. Blend the colors together.

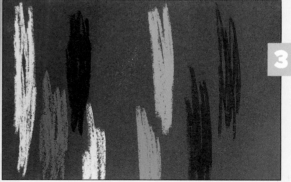

**5**

## Try This!

Get out your sidewalk chalk and draw a large picture outside on the pavement. Use layering, highlights, and shadows, just as you did in the aquarium exercise. Is it easier or harder to work with sidewalk chalk? If you like it, take a photo of your artwork before it gets washed away.

**6**

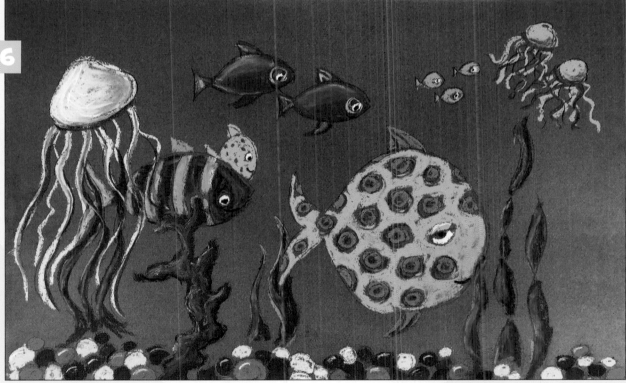

### JOHN SLOAN
(1871–1951) United States

Many artists use overlapping in their drawings, sketches, or paintings to create depth and an illusion of space. This painting by John Sloan called *South Beach Bathers* is a great example. Sloan became known for his drawings when he worked as an illustrator for magazines. In his artwork, he wanted to portray everyday life in a realistic way. For this beach scene, he used depth to make viewers feel like they could step right onto the sand and into the water. He overlapped people to give a sense of an inviting, close space—like the feeling of being together at a party.

*South Beach Bathers,* 1907-08

# THAT'S ONE PERSPECTIVE

Create the illusion of space by using one-point **perspective**. This technique gives a scene a 3-D look although the objects are drawn as flat and one-dimensional. The trick is to draw a line of objects that grow smaller as they lead toward a **vanishing point** where they disappear into the horizon. In this exercise, you will learn how to illustrate this in a drawing. This only works when looking directly at the subject or when looking directly down something long, like a road or railway track. When the subject is at an angle to you it becomes two-point or multiple perspective.

## You Will Need:
- Heavyweight paper
- Pencil and ruler
- Oil pastels
- Baby oil
- Brush

## PROJECT GUIDES

**1** Look at the photo to the right. Identify the horizon. Identify the point where the road seems to end. That is called the vanishing point because the object that is large and close to you seems to vanish in the distance.

**2** Using a pencil and light pressure, mark the vanishing point on your paper. Use a ruler and the pencil to draw a line across the horizon. Above and below the horizon draw a line from the vanishing point to each corner of the paper.

**3** Color the road with oil pastels. Use a lighter color in the foreground and a darker color near the vanishing point. Blend the colors together with your finger. Tones that go from light to dark make the road look like it is receding.

**4** Color the grass with oil pastels. Use light shades in the foreground and dark shades near the horizon. Blend the colors with your finger. Color the sky using light colors of oil pastels near the horizon and dark shades at the top of the page.

**5** Draw outlines of trees along the sides of the road. Each tree will be drawn from the bottom to the top of the guide lines. This will make the trees smaller as they get closer to the vanishing point. Fill in each outline with oil pastels.

**6** Draw in the road dividing line. Start with long dashes and make them shorter as they get close to the vanishing point.

**1**

**2**
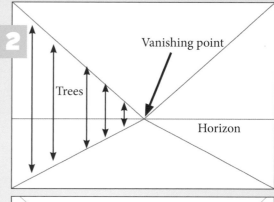

Vanishing point

Trees

Horizon

**3**
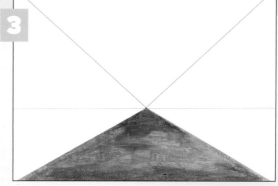

28

**4**

## Try This!

Draw your own scene with one-point perspective. It could be a landscape or an interior, such as a long hallway. Imagine what is at the vanishing point. Is it a beautiful flower garden? Or a scary ghost on Halloween? Use color and shading to give the viewer that feeling.

**5**

## Helpful Tip

● *To help with blending colors together, paint a little baby oil on your pastel drawing before rubbing the colors with your finger.*

**6**

## BOOKS

*Art for Kids: Drawing*
by Kathryn Temple, Sterling Children's Books, 2014.

*Draw 50 Animals*,
by Lee J. Ames, Watson-Guptill, 2012.

*The Children's Interactive Story of Art*
by Susie Hodge, Carlton Kids, 2016.

*How to Draw Cool Stuff*,
by Catherine V. Holmes, Library Tales Publishing, 2014.

## WEBSITES

### National Gallery of Art
**www.nga.gov/education/kids.html**
NGAkids Art Zone includes descriptions of interactive art-making tools that are free to download. You can also explore the collection at the National Gallery.

### Drawing for Kids
**www.artforkidshub.com/how-to-draw/**
This website features a large collection of videos on how to draw...anything.

### Art Projects—Drawing
**https://artprojectsforkids.org/category/view-by-theme/drawing-tutorials/**
This website features a great collection of drawing projects.

### Community Art Authority
**http://community.artauthority.net/Index.asp**
This website features a collection of works by major artists, from ancient times to today. They also have an app you can download.

# GLOSSARY

**3-D effect** A system or effect that adds a three-dimensional appearance to visual images

**alignment** The placement of visual elements so that they line up in a composition

**anatomy** The study of the structure of living things, such as bone and muscle

**complement** To add to something in a way that makes it better or more balanced

**contour** An outline, especially of a curving or irregular figure

**depth** The illusion of distance from front to back or near to far in an artwork

**doodling** An aimless or casual scribbling, or sketching

**foreground** The portion of a scene nearest to the viewer (opposed to background)

**hand-eye-mind coordination** The ability to do activities that require the use of our hands and eyes at the same time

**monochromatic** Having a single color

**negative space** The area not filled by the subject or subjects of an artwork

**non-dominant hand** The non-preferred hand; the left hand if you are right-handed, the right hand if you are left-handed

**parallel** Always the same distance apart and never touching

**perspective** A way of looking at something; in art, a technique for making a flat, two-dimensional surface look 3-D

**positive space** The area filled by the subject or subjects of an artwork

**primary colors** The colors which cannot be made from others, which are red, blue, and yellow

**proportion** The relationship of objects in an artwork based on their size

**realistic portrait** A portrait that represents the subject truthfully

**recede** To move back or away from a previous position

**Rubin's vase** An optical illusion created about 1915 by Danish psychologist Edgar Rubin, who was studying perception

**secondary colors** Colors which can be made from primary colors

**stippling** Creating patterns with small dots

**subject** The main idea that is represented in the artwork

**symmetry** Correct or pleasing proportion of the parts of a thing, especially an artwork

**techniques** The method and ability with which an artist uses technical skills to create art

**vanishing point** The spot on the horizon where receding lines meet and seem to disappear

**visualize** To form mental images or pictures in one's mind

**whorl** A pattern of spirals and/or circles

# INDEX

## ABOUT THE AUTHOR

Sandee Ewasiuk is a graduate of OCAD. She has participated in many group and solo exhibitions and her paintings can be found in corporate and private collections around the world. She currently divides her time between painting and teaching art at the Dundas Valley School of Art, The Art Gallery of Burlington, and Fleming College/Halliburton School of Art. She recently spent a month in Thailand as an artist-in-residence, exploring painting and mixed media. Sandee continues to experiment with and explore new ideas and techniques.